the little book of
CONFIDENCE

lucy lane

summersdale

THE LITTLE BOOK OF CONFIDENCE

Copyright © Summersdale Publishers Ltd, 2018

With research by Robert Drew

Star icon © Blan-k/Shutterstock.com

An Hachette UK Company
www.hachette.co.uk

Summersdale Publishers Ltd
Part of Octopus Publishing Group Limited
Carmelite House
50 Victoria Embankment
LONDON
EC4Y 0DZ
UK

www.summersdale.com

Printed and bound in the Czech Republic

ISBN: 978-1-78685-527-5

Substantial discounts on bulk quantities of Summersdale books are available to corporations, professional associations and other organisations. For details contact general enquiries: telephone: +44 (0) 1243 771107 or email: enquiries@summersdale.com.

INTRODUCTION

Everyone could use a confidence boost. Whether you're struggling with daily insecurities or looking to supercharge your self-belief, there are simple and practical steps you can take to improve your mood, soothe your mind and change your life for the better. This book is packed with easy-to-follow tips and encouraging quotes that will help you understand what real confidence is and what you can do today to build yours up and achieve your goals.

You have to believe
in yourself when
no one else does.

Venus Williams

OUR GREATEST GLORY IS NOT IN NEVER FALLING BUT IN RISING EVERY TIME WE FALL.

Oliver Goldsmith

SEE A MORE CONFIDENT YOU

When starting out on a journey of self-improvement, it can be difficult to see what the end result will be. It's easy to become bogged down in the 'what ifs' a situation brings to mind, and this is where visualisation can help. Sitting in a comfortable chair, in a relaxed position, close your eyes and begin to focus on your breathing. There is no need to breathe more slowly – just pay attention to your natural breathing patterns. Next, start to build a picture in your head of how a more confident 'you' would look and act. Where are you? Who is with you? Notice the details and enjoy the feeling of confidence growing from within. While you are working on building your confidence, take this image with you and use it as motivation to become this new, more confident, version of yourself.

WHERE ARE YOU CONFIDENT?

An important question to ask yourself is this: where do you feel most and least confident? This is not just a question of location – although for some people, certain places can affect how they feel emotionally. It's more about the areas of your life where you feel most or least at ease when it comes to confidence. Someone may, for instance, feel assured in their professional life, but lack confidence when it comes to personal relationships. Knowing which areas (both physical and emotional) affect your self-belief can help you to build your confidence levels. At first, situations or places that knock your confidence can be avoided if you feel you're already at a low point. Later, you can work on altering the way you perceive these situations using the helpful tips suggested in this book.

CHOOSE YOUR RESPONSE

We all experience lows and crises in our lives, but how we respond to these situations is up to us. When something 'bad' dents our confidence, we can choose to react negatively, or we can opt to remain calm and look for a solution. Often our first reactions are just habits we've fallen into, so it's important to realise that you always have a choice. When faced with a setback, pause for a moment and consciously decide how you would like to respond.

Believe and act as if it were impossible to fail.

Charles F. Kettering

KEEP A CONFIDENCE DIARY

To help you on your journey to greater confidence, write down what you're going through and record when your confidence is at its highest or lowest points. Choose a notebook that reflects your personality; whether it's a simple notepad or an illustrated diary, you are more likely to use something you like the look of. Keep it where you will use it – by the bed, near your favourite spot on the sofa or wherever you will notice it. The act of writing down how you feel, and what your confidence levels are like from day to day, will help you keep track of the events or situations that knock your self-belief. However, remember to record the high points as well as the lows: the diary will give you something to look back at during darker days to remind you that things will get better.

You have to expect things of yourself before you can do them.

Michael Jordan

BE SHOCKING,
BE DARING,
BE BOLD,
BE PASSIONATE.

Jane Porter

GET COMFORTABLE BEING UNCOMFORTABLE

Life can make you feel uncomfortable, but this doesn't have to stop you from achieving your goals. In fact, if you can become comfortable with feeling uncomfortable, you'll have the confidence to handle whatever situation comes your way. Unfortunately, most of us avoid discomfort. We live within small, familiar comfort zones that limit what we do in our lives. When you regularly take risks, however, your comfort zone expands. Even taking small steps towards your goals can expand your horizons and make you feel more positive about life. Remember, feeling uncomfortable can be a good sign – it means that you're moving forwards and exploring unfamiliar territory, and in return you'll be more open to new people, places, experiences and adventures in your life.

I ALWAYS DID SOMETHING I WAS A LITTLE NOT READY TO DO.

Marissa Mayer

Life **begins** at the end of your **comfort zone**.

Neale Donald Walsch

SET GOALS FOR YOURSELF

Goal-setting is the key to success, and therefore to confidence-building. You may want to set small goals at first to help break down bigger tasks into more manageable pieces, or it may be that you have long-term aims that you want to make reality. The most important thing, no matter how big or small the goal, is that it suits your needs, lifestyle and interests. Your goal can be related to any aspect of your life. Do you want to learn to paint? Travel somewhere exotic? Learn a language? Now is the time to start! If you choose to do something because you feel you 'should', or because it is the socially acceptable goal for someone in your current position, the chances are you won't have the motivation to make it all the way. Instead, make sure your aims reflect what you really want; you'll see how much better you work towards them.

DO NOT THINK OF TODAY'S FAILURES, BUT OF THE SUCCESS THAT MAY COME TOMORROW.

Helen Keller

Courage is not the absence of fear, but rather the judgement that something else is more important than fear.

Meg Cabot

IT'S A JOURNEY

It might sound like a cliché, but think of the process of gaining confidence as a journey. It won't happen overnight, and there may be ups and downs along the way, but you will get to your destination if you keep going. Remember to look back from time to time to see how far you've come.

When you come
to a **roadblock,**
take a **detour.**

Mary Kay Ash

GET SMART ABOUT YOUR GOALS

When you have identified which goals will make you happy, try this further step to help you work towards them. A positive way to ensure that your goals will work for you is by making them SMART (specific, measurable, attainable, relevant and time-bound). This can be applied to goals relating to any aspect of your life – they don't have to be work-related. SMART goals mean that: (S) you should know exactly what it is you want to achieve; (M) you should be able to measure your progress; (A) it should be possible for you to achieve it, though not too easy; (R) it should relate to your wider goals; and (T) you should know when you'll want to have reached your goal.

IT IS CONFIDENCE IN OUR BODIES, MINDS AND SPIRITS THAT ALLOWS US TO KEEP LOOKING FOR NEW ADVENTURES.

Oprah Winfrey

We could spend our
life being afraid of
the hypothetical or
we can just be brave
and live life anyway.

Dolly Mahtani

ZOOM OUT

Whenever your confidence takes a bump and you need a quick and simple pick-me-up, take a mental step back for a moment. Think about the problem in the bigger story of your life. Will it still matter in a week, a month, or a year from now? Many of the things we worry about cease to matter after a while, so zooming out like this helps to speed up the process of building confidence by giving you some instant perspective.

A ship in harbour
is safe, but that
is not what ships
are built for.

John A. Shedd

LET GO OF 'PERFECT'

Improving your confidence, and so your life overall, is a noble goal. However, it's important to remember that there is no endpoint. Even when you reach the goals that you have set for yourself, new ones will take their place. Plus, no matter how long or hard you work at something, it will never be completely perfect – and that's OK. Accepting this fact of life will set you free to enjoy the process of making progress.

It takes courage to grow up and become who you really are.

E. E. Cummings

DON'T TAKE THINGS TOO SERIOUSLY

It's good to be motivated and focused, but you needn't lose your sense of humour along the way. If you suffer any kind of setback, whether it's a late train or a bad date, try to find something funny about the situation. When you decide not to take things too seriously, these frustrations will lose a lot of their power to derail you. On difficult days, laughter is the best medicine for the soul.

YOU CAN STEER YOURSELF IN ANY DIRECTION YOU CHOOSE.

Dr Seuss

TAKE TIME TO UNPLUG

For all its benefits in connecting us to friends and loved ones, social media can be toxic to confidence. While it undoubtedly allows us to share happiness and positivity with those around us, it also remains open to abuse by those who want to brag about themselves or to bring others down. Rather than comparing your life and achievements with those of others (which, don't forget, have been artfully presented online), take some steps to reduce the time you spend engaging with them. Try unfollowing people you may barely know or like, or even deleting the most addictive apps from your phone. When you take a break from all the online hubbub, you'll be able to focus on who and what is truly important to you in real life.

YOU HAVE POWER OVER YOUR MIND – NOT OUTSIDE EVENTS. REALISE THIS, AND YOU WILL FIND STRENGTH.

Marcus Aurelius

Your **self-worth**
is defined by **you**. You
don't have to depend
on someone telling you
who you are.

Beyoncé

CHERISH COMPLIMENTS

Receiving genuine compliments can boost your self-esteem – so don't brush them off. Thank the person who has paid you the compliment and take a moment to internalise what has just been said. In the same way, savour any words of praise from family, friends and work colleagues. Save positive emails, cards and messages, and file away your best performance reviews at work. Read these words of praise whenever you need a quick shot of encouragement and confidence.

Always be a
first-rate version of
yourself, instead of a
second-rate version
of somebody else.

Judy Garland

PRACTISE MINDFULNESS

Mindfulness, which has developed from Buddhist teachings, is a technique for living in the here and now, rather than being preoccupied with the past or the future. It can help you reduce your stress levels by allowing you to let go of obsessive thoughts about what's been and gone, or what is yet to happen. A simple technique to increase your mindfulness is to alter your route to work slightly so that you pay more attention to your surroundings, rather than being 'on autopilot'. Taking time to reflect on your environment can put your worries into perspective, where they might otherwise have preoccupied you and caused you stress. If you can be mindful, you will be able to pay more attention to the positive aspects of your day and gain confidence from seeing them more clearly in the present moment.

HAVE THE COURAGE TO FOLLOW YOUR HEART AND INTUITION.

Steve Jobs

If you **ask me** what I
came into this life to do,
I will tell you: I came
to **live out loud**.

Émile Zola

STOP COMPARING YOURSELF

The desire to do and be better is a positive trait. But continually striving for a perceived version of perfection can stop you from being happy with who you already are and prevent you from seeing all the positive things in your life. A common perfectionist tendency is to compare yourself to others. This may either take the form of direct comparison, such as, 'Sarah is more successful in her job than I am,' or of general comparison along the lines of, 'I wish I could be more like Ben.' Either way, in seeing others as somehow better than you, you are moving your focus away from your own positives. In trying to be like other people, you stop yourself from being the best version of you. Instead, think about the areas of your life you would like to improve, and then work on those. Everybody starts from different points in life, which makes comparison pointless: what matters is that you are making progress on a path you have chosen for yourself.

Don't compare yourself with anyone in this world. If you do so, you are insulting yourself.

Bill Gates

WHY SHOULD I CARE WHAT OTHER PEOPLE THINK OF ME? I AM WHO I AM. AND WHO I WANNA BE.

Avril Lavigne

FEEDBACK, NOT FAILURE

It's possible that even if you set the most relevant, realistic goals, you may not achieve them in the way or within the timeframe you would like. Life may throw something unexpected in your path that stops you from achieving what you want, when you want, but always remember: this is not failure. Feeling like you have failed is bound to knock your confidence. The best thing to do is to draw a mental line under it, learn from what's happened and try again. The right f-word to use here is 'feedback': this is what any experience gives you to help you improve next time. As long as you are still trying, you are working towards your long-term goals – and as long as you are doing that, you will never fail.

Only those who dare to **fail greatly,** can ever **achieve greatly.**

Robert F. Kennedy

IF YOU LEARN FROM DEFEAT, YOU HAVEN'T REALLY LOST.

Zig Ziglar

WORK ON WEAKNESSES

It can be tempting to avoid addressing any areas of your life where you're not completely confident. But you'll never feel better about this unless you honestly identify these difficulties and invest time and effort in looking at them. Take a step today, however small, to improve one of your less-developed skills. If you want to be less shy, say, make small talk with the barista when you next get a coffee. It might just brighten their day – and yours!

We must accept finite
disappointment, but
never lose infinite hope.

Martin Luther King Jr

If you're walking down the **right path** and you're willing to keep walking, eventually you'll make **progress**.

Barack Obama

I DON'T THINK LIMITS.

Usain Bolt

WALK TALL

The thought of exercise can be daunting, especially if your confidence is low. Joining a gym or going to a group class can seem like the last thing you would want to do. But exercise can be as simple as going for a walk. Just one 30-minute stroll each day can significantly improve your health and emotional well-being. You could fit this in on the way to work, at lunchtime, or whenever feels right for you. The best walks are in daylight, in natural surroundings. Not only will being outdoors offer you a natural boost, helping you feel better and lifting your spirits, but the exercise itself will also produce endorphins, making you feel great. If you happen to see your body shape improving too, that's bound to give your confidence an extra lift.

BE UNIQUE.
BE MEMORABLE.
BE CONFIDENT.
BE PROUD.

Shannon L. Alder

I often find it's just the confidence that makes you sexy; not what your body looks like.

Queen Latifah

STAY HYDRATED

As well as being essential for good health, keeping hydrated is good for your self-esteem as it helps your skin and hair look their best, boosting body confidence. Water also helps to flush out your system, keeping your bowels healthy and reducing feelings of bloating or puffiness. Drinking around two litres of water each day (more than this when you exercise) is generally recommended for optimum health.

You are **braver**
than you believe,
stronger than you
seem, and **smarter**
than you think.

A. A. Milne

If you're presenting
yourself with confidence,
you can pull off pretty
much anything.

Katy Perry

DON'T QUIT. SUFFER NOW AND LIVE THE REST OF YOUR LIFE AS A CHAMPION.

Muhammad Ali

MASTER A MARTIAL ART

When you first start to exercise, you may want to opt for something gentle that doesn't put too much strain on your body, such as walking or swimming. But if you are feeling more adventurous, martial arts could help you to build your self-image in several ways. To start with, practising martial arts is more strenuous and can therefore help you to become stronger and fitter much faster than gentle exercise. What's more, martial arts teach self-control, and progressing within the discipline makes you more able to defend yourself, which can provide a confidence boost. There are many types of martial art to choose from, whether it's a 'softer' style, such as aikido, or something 'harder' like taekwondo. Each has its own individual benefits: find one that suits you.

THE FIRST STEP IS YOU HAVE TO SAY THAT YOU CAN.

Will Smith

The question isn't
who is going to
let me; it's who is
going to **stop me**?

Ayn Rand

DANCE FOR JOY

Dancing is one of the most fun ways to keep fit, and it releases plenty of feel-good endorphins, too. It can be as simple as putting on your favourite tunes at home and dancing around the room, or you could try a class. Jive, jazz and salsa classes are all great ways to get fit and meet new people, and fitness fusion classes such as Zumba are also very popular. Getting fitter and better at your chosen style is a sure-fire confidence boost.

Confidence comes from other places, not just how you look.

Darcey Bussell

GIVE 'GREEN EXERCISE' A GO

Gyms are great during cold and gloomy winter months, but they can get a bit repetitive after a while. You can easily freshen up the task of keeping fit by embracing the great outdoors. 'Green exercise' is any physical activity undertaken outside in natural surroundings – it can be as simple as spending more time jogging around your garden, strolling through a local park or venturing into nearby woods. Simply being in the great outdoors and breathing in the bracing fresh air can bring a real sense of peace and tranquillity. Whether it's along the coast, through fields, or even just in your own backyard, exercising outdoors can also improve your mood, ease muscle tension and lower blood pressure – and getting closer to nature may give you the boost you need to feel calm under pressure, balanced, content and, overall, more confident.

SMILE!

The simple act of smiling releases endorphins, the body's natural feel-good drug – and studies have shown that a person's mood begins to reflect the emotion that their face is communicating. So even if you don't feel like it, turning up the corners of your mouth into a smile will not only boost your mood, it will make you appear friendly and confident to those around you. Win–win!

Never dull your **shine**
for **somebody else.**

Tyra Banks

CUT OUT COMFORT EATING

When you feel down, it can be easy to reach for a favourite food to give you a lift. Comfort eating, however, is likely to only make the situation worse. The urge to comfort eat comes from the 'fight or flight' stress reaction, which is ingrained in us despite not being that relevant to modern lifestyles. When we feel bad about ourselves, we tend to be stressed. This leads our bodies to believe we are under attack, and that we will either have to face up to the attacker (fight) or run away (flight). Both of these options require extra energy that can be used quickly – and this means sugar! However, the sugar boost won't last very long and eating that extra slice of cake probably won't help you feel better. If you get a snack attack, try eating some fruit instead and you'll feel the physical and emotional benefits.

Change your
thoughts and you
change the world.

Norman Vincent Peale

Act as if
what you do
makes a difference.
It does.

William James

TAKE A BREAK FROM BOOZE

When we're feeling low, for example after a hard day at work, or when we're lacking confidence in a social situation, many of us will reach for a drink to help us relax. Alcohol does have an instantly calming effect, but this is cancelled out by the depressant qualities of booze, and the feeling of anxiety that can be left behind once the effects wear off. Also, contrary to the popular idea of a 'nightcap', alcohol can disturb your sleep. To feel your best, try to cut down on your drinking as much as possible and if you do go for a tipple, opt for a small glass of Chianti, Merlot or Cabernet Sauvignon. These wines are abundant in procyanidins, plant chemicals which are beneficial to health – especially to our cardiovascular health. They are also rich in melatonin, the sleep hormone, which is good news because a well-rested person is more likely to be a confident person.

You have to be unique
and different and shine
in your own way.

Lady Gaga

YOU CAN,
YOU SHOULD,
AND IF YOU'RE
BRAVE ENOUGH
TO START,
YOU WILL.

Stephen King

A THOUGHT IS JUST A THOUGHT

We have thousands of thoughts every day. Most will be unexceptional, but some are significant and can be harmful – such as thinking to yourself, 'I'm not good enough.' Repeating negative thoughts can have a detrimental effect on your confidence levels, but once you recognise this negativity as simply a thought with no substance, you can begin to challenge it and rebuild your self-concept. Recognise that your thoughts do not need to control the way you feel and behave.

We **are** what we
believe we are.

C. S. Lewis

CLOTHE YOURSELF IN CONFIDENCE

If your current wardrobe leaves something to be desired, now might be the time to refresh it with clothes that flatter you and make you feel good. The way you dress affects the way you feel – there's wisdom in the old adage that says 'dress for the job you want, not the one you have'. Choose well-fitted clothes that reflect your personality. Make sure that when you look in the mirror, you think, 'Yes, I look good today,' rather than, 'What am I wearing?' or, 'It will have to do.' Feeling good in your clothes will make you feel more comfortable in your own skin; this will boost your confidence levels – both in the workplace and beyond.

THE MOST BEAUTIFUL THING YOU CAN WEAR IS CONFIDENCE.

Blake Lively

You need to believe
in yourself and what
you do. Be tenacious
and genuine.

Christian Louboutin

COLOUR ME CONFIDENT

As well as choosing the right styles and cuts, your new wardrobe should be full of colours which suit your skin tone and heighten your mood. Yellow is said to make you feel happier, blue is meant to calm and red is a well-known 'power colour'. If you're more of a monochrome fan, you can still add a pop of colour through accessories, like a scarf, tie or hat.

We are all of us
stars, and we deserve
to **twinkle**.

Marilyn Monroe

The most courageous
act is still to think
for yourself. Aloud.

Coco Chanel

ATTITUDE IS A LITTLE THING THAT MAKES A BIG DIFFERENCE.

Winston Churchill

THE SCENT OF SUCCESS

Fragrances matter: not only do they make you smell good, but they have been proven to enhance confidence. And when you smell good, you feel more attractive and better about yourself, too. Find a scent that suits your personality – something that lifts you the instant you spritz it on. Choose from four fragrance groups: floral and fruity; fresh and zesty; woody and musky; or oriental and spicy. Consider layering your scent by using soap, shower gels and body lotions with similar or complementary scents.

Be unapologetically
you.

Steve Maraboli

LET YOUR BODY TALK

A significant proportion of the way we communicate is done purely through body language. Before you say even a single word, you are speaking volumes through your posture, eye contact and other physical gestures. Make the most of this by consciously adjusting your body language to convey confidence. Stand tall or sit up straight, with your shoulders back and your chin up. Avoid crossing your arms, so that you appear open rather than confrontational. Try not to fiddle with your hair or clothing, and don't bite your nails or lips as this communicates that you're feeling unsettled. Make regular eye contact with the person you're speaking to, and nod gently to offer positive reinforcement. At first it might feel unusual to focus on your body language like this, but over time these behaviours will come to feel natural, making a big difference to how other people perceive you – and how you perceive yourself.

WITH CONFIDENCE, YOU HAVE WON BEFORE YOU HAVE STARTED.

Marcus Garvey

Whatever we expect
with confidence
becomes our own
self-fulfilling prophecy.

Brian Tracy

MAKE USE OF A MANTRA

Mantras are positive words or phrases that you repeat to yourself, either out loud or in your head. Many people find mantras a powerful way of stopping negative trains of thought. If you find yourself regularly thinking, 'I can't', your mantra could be as simple as, 'I can do this' or, 'Nothing can stop me.' Develop and use a mantra of your own to repeat whenever worry or doubt try to distract you.

If you are going to
doubt something,
doubt your **limits**.

Don Ward

ASK!

Sometimes we all forget the wisdom contained in the line, 'If you don't ask, you don't get.' Confident and successful people go for what they want and seek to get what they think they deserve. Whether it's a date or a pay rise, the worst that can happen is that you get a 'no', but until you ask the question, you'll never truly know the answer. Instead of assuming, go and find out!

Your chances of success
in any undertaking can
always be measured by
your belief in yourself.

Robert Collier

FIND YOUR CONFIDENT VOICE

When speaking in public or to colleagues at work, your voice is a key communicator of confidence – or lack of it. If you're nervous, your voice can sound squeaky and high-pitched and you might talk very quickly, which signals insecurity to those listening. Instead, cultivate a deeper, calmer, slower speaking voice. Breathe in deeply and breathe out from your stomach. This will help your voice to vibrate and resonate. Also, try to imagine your voice to be warm and 'chocolatey', flowing smoothly from your lips. This rich and unrushed manner will put your audience immediately at ease, allowing you to win them over with your tone of voice as well as your line of argument.

Life is a
hell of a lot more
fun if you say 'yes'
rather than '**no**'.

Richard Branson

BELIEVE YOU CAN AND YOU'RE HALFWAY THERE.

Theodore Roosevelt

BE ASSERTIVE

When you're lacking confidence, it can seem like an easier option to bow to the wishes of others and say 'yes' to everything, even if you're not actually happy with the situation. Though it seems like the simplest option, doing this in fact negatively affects your confidence, as you are essentially telling yourself that the wishes of others are more important than your own. Being assertive doesn't have to mean being aggressive. The main thing is that you realise your own needs are as important as everybody else's. Consider this simple scenario: your boss asks you to take on a new project when you are already overworked and you know that you will not be able to finish it to the necessary standard. Instead of taking it on because you think it's the correct thing to do, explain the situation to your boss so that a solution can be found. The likelihood is that, at the very least, they will appreciate your honesty.

A GREAT FIGURE OR PHYSIQUE IS NICE, BUT IT'S SELF-CONFIDENCE THAT MAKES SOMEONE REALLY SEXY.

Vivica A. Fox

Courage isn't having
the strength to go on –
it is going on when you
don't have strength.

Napoleon Bonaparte

ACT AS THOUGH YOU HAVE AMPLE CONFIDENCE

Vividly imagine what your life would be like if you were fully confident right now. How would your posture be? How would your voice sound? What would you say to yourself? Once you have a clear image, imagine you are this person. Step into their shoes and see the world through their eyes – feel what they feel. If you do this enough you'll forget that you're only acting, and feeling confident will become normal and natural for you.

Aerodynamically the **bumblebee** shouldn't be able to **fly**, but the bumblebee doesn't know so it goes on **flying** anyway.

Mary Kay Ash

MAKE EYE CONTACT

People who make strong eye contact are seen as being more trustworthy and positive. However, connecting with someone's gaze can feel uncomfortable if you are shy or feeling nervous. In that case, try fixing your gaze between the other person's eyes. They won't be able to tell you're not looking them directly in the eyes and you'll give the impression of being self-assured. Just make sure to avert your gaze briefly every so often to avoid giving them an intimidating stare!

BELIEVE IN YOUR FLYNESS AND CONQUER YOUR SHYNESS.

Kanye West

Throw caution to the
wind and just do it.

Carrie Underwood

Confidence

comes with maturity,
being more **accepting**
of yourself.

Nicole Scherzinger

FOCUS ON WHAT YOU CAN DO

Before any high-pressure event, like an exam or a presentation, your confidence can dip and nerves can get the better of you if you dwell on what you are lacking in that moment. But at this point, there's nothing more to be done, so it does you no good to agonise over it. Instead, focus your thoughts on what you have prepared and on what you *do* know, rather than all the things you don't. Do the best with what you have.

It always seems
impossible until
it is done.

Nelson Mandela

HOW DOES THIS HELP ME?

Having the right frame of mind means you can find the positives in any situation. When faced with a problem, ask yourself this counterintuitive question: 'How does this *help* me?' Maybe a challenge at work forces you to develop a new skill. Or perhaps breaking up with someone frees you to focus on your own needs for a while. Silver linings will always appear to you if you look for them.

Opportunities **multiply** as they are **seized.**

Sun Tzu

MODEL BEHAVIOUR

A clever way to improve self-confidence is to model the habits of highly confident people. Choose a role model who is highly competent in the area where you would like more confidence – whether that's giving a presentation at work or going on dates – and model as many of their behaviours, attitudes and habits as possible. If you have the chance to talk to them, ask them about their attitudes and thought processes. If the person is a well-known figure, you can learn from them by reading their books or biographies and studying their TV shows, films or interviews. At first, it may feel unnatural to act differently, but there's wisdom in the motto 'fake it until you make it'; in time you'll internalise the confident mindsets and behaviours to the point where it's no longer a conscious performance.

IN ORDER TO SUCCEED, WE MUST FIRST BELIEVE THAT WE CAN.

Nikos Kazantzakis

Go confidently in
the direction of your
dreams. Live the life
you've imagined.

Henry David Thoreau

REST IS BEST

Sleep is a crucial foundation of your overall health, well-being and confidence levels. Understanding how much sleep is normal for you is the first step to getting better-quality shut-eye. Many of us lie awake at night worrying that we won't get the recommended eight hours' sleep that we need to function well. However, studies have shown that most people will have no problem functioning with six or seven hours' sleep – and what's more, many people find that if they have lost sleep, they only need to catch up on about one-third of the lost time to feel better. For example, if you went to bed an hour-and-a-half late one night of the week, a 30-minute lie-in at the weekend should do the trick. Changing our perceptions of how long we need to sleep can help us: feel more secure, and therefore help us sleep more easily; achieve better quality sleep; feel more rested; and get ready to take on new challenges with a more positive outlook.

Don't waste your energy trying to change opinions... **do your thing** and **don't care** if they like it.

Tina Fey

BELIEVE WITH ALL YOUR HEART THAT YOU WILL DO WHAT YOU WERE MADE TO DO.

Orison Swett Marden

LEARN SOMETHING NEW

Whether it's taking driving lessons, learning a new language or discovering a new hobby, becoming skilled at something new can lead to increased self-esteem. Admittedly, it takes courage to be a beginner at something and to acquire new skills, but the satisfaction of venturing out of your comfort zone and being able to do something well can make you feel really good about yourself. Is there an instrument you have always wanted to play or a sport you fancy trying? Perhaps you might prefer to learn something practical like baking or gardening? Research shows that people who continue to learn throughout their lives are more optimistic and have a higher sense of self-worth. Plus, going to a class is a great way to enhance your social life.

Through my
education, I didn't
just develop skills,
I didn't just develop the
ability to learn, but I
developed confidence.

Michelle Obama

NO ONE KNOWS WHAT HE CAN DO UNTIL HE TRIES.

Publilius Syrus

ASK YOURSELF 'WHY?'

One of the key ways to challenge negative thoughts that can drain your confidence is to ask a very simple question: 'Why?' For example, the negative thought that a lot of us wrestle with – 'I'm not good enough' – can make you worried about many aspects of your life. Perhaps you feel you are not good enough at your job, not a good enough friend, or not a good enough parent. Now is the time to ask yourself why that is: can you find five legitimate reasons why you are not good enough? It's unlikely you can. Let reason prevail; if the only way you can answer this simple question is with 'because I know it's true' or by citing minor incidents from the past, it's time to change your self-perception.

STAY HUMBLE

As your confidence grows, so might your ego. With each milestone reached and goal achieved, there is a risk that your self-belief could spill over into arrogance or actually overconfidence. Watch out for this and the way you come across to others. Though it may be tempting to brag about success, humility is a far healthier attitude in the long-term. Be confident, by all means, but also be kind.

As soon as you **trust yourself**, you will know how to **live**.

Johann Wolfgang von Goethe

USE YOUR IMAGINATION

Your brain and body can't tell the difference between something you vividly imagine and something that's real. That's why your mouth waters when you imagine biting into a slice of chocolate cake. You can use this to your advantage if you're feeling nervous about doing something for the first time, such as giving a speech. By closing your eyes and repeatedly imagining yourself wildly succeeding, you create neural pathways in your brain which programme you to perform well the next time you give a speech in real life. In order for this to be effective, you need to run your mental movie repeatedly and engage all your senses, so that the scenario is as vivid and realistic as possible. Picture your surroundings, hear the sound of your voice, see the audience respond enthusiastically and feel the excitement and confidence growing inside you.

LIFE SHRINKS OR EXPANDS IN PROPORTION TO ONE'S COURAGE.

Anaïs Nin

Imaginary obstacles
are insurmountable.
Real ones aren't.

Barbara Sher

COUNT YOUR BLESSINGS

When times are tough – and even when things are just peachy – make a habit of listing the good things in your life: actually write them down. This simple act of gratitude, especially before you go to sleep, will soothe your soul. Whether it's health, family, friends, your job or your partner, recognise and dwell awhile on your blessings.

The **essential lesson** I've learned in life is to just **be yourself**. Treasure the **magnificent** being that you are.

Wayne Dyer

MIX WITH POSITIVE PEOPLE

Spending time with upbeat, supportive people rubs off on you and puts you in a positive frame of mind. Smiles and laughter are wonderfully infectious. Your friends are an obvious source of this great energy. They can build you up and improve your self-confidence and self-worth. True friends support your efforts to achieve your goals – they celebrate your successes and console you when things don't go according to plan. They're also a sounding board for ideas and can provide a valuable second opinion.

Sadly, not all friends are like this, and if the people you mix with tend to drain you or bring you down a lot, it's time to find some new pals. However, even strong friendships will go through rough patches, so don't give up on someone because of one argument or minor disagreement. Remember to be a good friend yourself and you will attract similarly sweet souls.

NO ONE
CAN MAKE YOU
FEEL INFERIOR
WITHOUT YOUR
CONSENT.

Eleanor Roosevelt

It's just better to be yourself than to try to be some version of what you think the other person wants.

Matt Damon

CONFIDENCE IS PREPARATION

When the pressure of deadlines, meetings, phone calls and long hours builds up, we doubt our ability to stay on top of things. In turn, this causes a dip in confidence. Unfortunately, not only does this get in the way of an effective and satisfying working life, but it can also have a knock-on effect on your personal life. Perhaps the simplest way to reduce this feeling of pressure is to plan and prepare in advance. Pack your lunch the night before so that you're not rushing to put it together in the morning. Choose your outfit, so that you're not delayed by deciding what to wear. Make a list of the tasks you want to complete, so that when you get to your place of work, or to school, your day is already mapped out. Of course, there will be times when your planning is disrupted by unexpected events, and you will have to adapt, but taking these preliminary steps will give you a firm foundation of confidence that your day is set up to go well.

You only get **one chance** at life and you have to **grab it boldly**.

Bear Grylls

IF YOU HAVE AN IDEA, YOU HAVE TO BELIEVE IN YOURSELF OR NO ONE ELSE WILL.

Sarah Michelle Gellar

MOOD MUSIC

The power of music to influence our mood is undeniable, and today we have the advantage of being able to carry around huge libraries of tracks in our pockets. Make a mood-boosting 'confidence playlist' with your own choice of tunes that make you feel fantastic. Then, whenever you're faced with a difficult day or a challenging situation, fire up those songs for some instant inspiration and motivation.

Doubt kills more dreams
than failure ever will.

Suzy Kassem

AVOID 'CATCHING' STRESS

When you spend extended periods of time with others, their moods and attitudes can affect yours. For example, a large amount of workplace stress is so-called 'second-hand' stress. If someone at work is feeling hassled, you can unconsciously absorb their feelings of negativity. To avoid this, for instance if a colleague is talking about work or personal problems, try to say something positive about the subject or offer them some advice. If they carry on, perhaps go to make a hot drink, or, if you cannot walk away, make sure you stay positive and try your best not to adopt your colleague's mindset. It takes faith in yourself to resist a colleague's negativity, and this can increase your confidence by showing you that you are capable of taking up such a challenge.

If we are facing the
right direction,
all we have to do is
keep on walking.

Buddhist proverb

IN MY MOMENTS
OF DOUBT, I'VE
TOLD MYSELF
FIRMLY: IF NOT
ME, WHO? IF NOT
NOW, WHEN?

Emma Watson

IT'S OK TO SEEK HELP

If confidence issues are having a sustained negative effect on your day-to-day life and none of the advice in this book seems to be helping, it is worth talking to a medical professional. There may or may not be an undiagnosed reason for your difficulties, and a doctor might recommend some kind of therapy or medication. Remember, it's not a sign of weakness to seek help and expert advice; in fact, it takes strength to confront your issues in this way.

Never give in.
Never give in.
Never, never,
never, never.

Winston Churchill

If you're interested in finding out more about our books, find us on Facebook at Summersdale Publishers and follow us on Twitter at @Summersdale.

www.summersdale.com